Anin RECORD BREAKERS

JOHN TOWNSEND

Badger Publishing Limited
Oldmedow Road,
Hardwick Industrial Estate,
King's Lynn PE30 4JJ
Telephone: 01438 791037

www.badgerlearning.co.uk

2 4 6 8 10 9 7 5 3 1

Animal Record Breakers ISBN 978-1-78147-537-9

Publisher: Susan Ross
Senior Editor: Danny Pearson
Designer: Fiona Grant

Photos: Cover image: REX/Mint images
Page 5: Image Broker/REX
Page 6: FLPA/REX
Page 9: Design Pics inc/REX
Page 11: Christopher Swann/Splashdown/REX
Page 13: Mint Images/REX
Page 14: Image Broker/REX
Page 15: Kaldari
Page 16: Mint Images/REX
Page 17: FLPA/REX
Page 18: Image Broker/REX
Page 19: Design Pics inc/REX
Page 21: REX/Monkey Business Images
Page 22: REX/Monkey Business Images
Page 23: Sunset/REX
Page 24: FLPA/REX
Page 25: REX/Nature Picture Library
Page 26: Vesa Moilanen/REX
Page 27: Kevin Scott Ramos
Page 28: Mike Maloney/REX

Attempts to contact all copyright holders have been made.
If any omitted would care to contact Badger Learning, we will be happy to make appropriate arrangements.

Animal RECORD BREAKERS

Contents

Badger
L E A R N I N G

1. Super-fast

Record breakers

Humans can be amazing. Athletes with super-fit bodies keep breaking records. Some can run at nearly 28 miles per hour. That's super-fast!

Even super-fit athletes can't catch up with the animal world. Many animals run faster, jump higher or leap further than any human.

They can out-perform us in many ways. In fact, some animal records might surprise you. But not all the animals in this book are super-fit. Some break other records – scary ones.

Get ready for a few shocks!

Runners on land

The cheetah is the fastest land animal in the world.

This super-beast zooms off faster than a sports car – 0 to almost 60mph (96km/h) in under three seconds. Cheetahs can sprint at 70mph (112km/h) in short bursts.

Usain Bolt wouldn't stand a chance!

Air power

The fastest bird on the planet is the peregrine falcon.
This bird of prey swoops down from a great height.
It reaches speeds of over 200 miles an hour (322km/h).
Then its talons slam into a victim, such as a pigeon.
A peregrine falcon can spot a pigeon from over five
miles away.

This super-falcon lives across Europe
and in western Asia.

Runner-up

The white-throated needletail (also called the spine-tailed swift or storm-bird) is the fastest flying bird (not diving).

Check out these speeds:

1. Peregrine falcon (diving)
321-563km/h
(200-350mph)

2. White-throated needletail
170km/h
(105mph)

3. Spur-winged goose
104km/h
(65mph)

A bird's heart beats 400 times per minute while resting and at up to 1000 beats per minute when flying.

Water power

The world's fastest fish can shoot through the sea at speeds of up to 70mph (112km/h). It is the sailfish, which raises the sail on its back to help it steer through the water. Groups of sailfish often hunt sardines. They do it in short bursts at great speed.

Sailfish grow bigger than humans – to over 3.4 metres long and weighing 100kg.

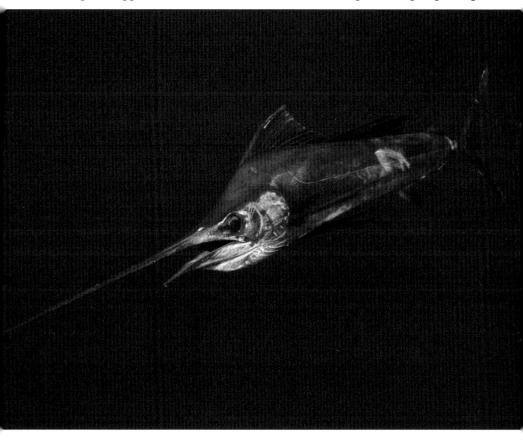

Fast fish league table

		(km/h)	(mph)
1. Sailfish		110	68
2. Marlin		80	50
3. Wahoo		78	48
4. Tunny		74	46
5. Bluefin tuna		70	44

WOW! facts

In 2005, a great white shark entered the record books. Named Nicole by scientists, this shark swam 12,400 miles (20,000 kilometres) from Africa to Australia in nine months. This was the longest and fastest journey recorded by any fish on the planet. Nicole was a real record breaker.

2. Super-wow

The animal that breaks many Wow! records is the blue whale. For size alone, it is a winner. At 30 metres long (that's two buses) and at 200 tons (15 buses), blue whales are even bigger than the biggest dinosaurs that ever lived.

Super size

Blue whales are found in all the world's oceans. They feed on tiny sea creatures called krill, which they filter out of the sea. That's 3-4 tons of krill a day for each blue whale.

A blue whale's tongue is as heavy as an elephant. Its heart alone is as heavy as a car. About 100 people can fit in a blue whale's mouth. But it might be best not to try!

WOW! facts

The blue whale is the loudest animal on Earth. Its call is louder than a jet engine!

Super strong

If you could carry six double-decker buses full of people, you would be as strong as the rhinoceros beetle! This beetle can carry 850 times its own body weight on its back. Even the mighty African elephant can only carry 25 per cent of its own weight. With around 100,000 muscles in its trunk, an elephant can lift up four humans – but that's nothing compared to the rhinoceros beetle. It might be small, but it's packed with power.

Rhinoceros beetles get their name from the tiny horn at the front of the male's head. This mighty beetle reaches 6-9 centimetres and holds the record for super strength.

Elephants are big lifters, but for its size the rhinoceros beetle wins the prize!

Super jumps

Fleas are well known for jumping – sometimes as far as 30cm in one hop. That's a bit like you leaping over eight buses. But another insect has also jumped into the record books.

The froghopper (also called a spittle bug) is only 6 millimetres long but it can ping itself 70 centimetres into the air. That's the same as you hopping over a skyscraper.

The froghopper

High jumpers

In 1993, Javier Sotomayor from Cuba won the high jump world record when he cleared 2.45 metres. That's nothing to a red kangaroo. Kangaroos have been known to jump fences over 3 metres high when trying to escape!

Long jumpers

American Mike Powell set the world long jump record when he leapt 8.95 metres. Big cats can do even better. A snow leopard holds the animal record for the longest jump when it leapt over a ditch that was 15 metres wide.

Fastest swimmers

When American Michael Phelps set the world swimming record, his speed in the water was 6.5km/h (4mph). That's not a patch on penguins. The Gentoo penguin can reach speeds of 35km/h (22mph) under water.

Maybe it's time to hold the first ever Animal Olympics!

3. Super survivors

Bird superstars

The Arctic tern is a marathon flyer. It survives a non-stop flight across the world and back each year. These birds fly from the Arctic to the Antarctic and back again. That's a round trip of 43,000 miles (70,000km). They have to stock up on food to build up their fat before they migrate.

Another seabird, called the sooty shearwater, is a close second to the tern. These birds migrate nearly 40,000 miles (64,000km) a year. They fly from New Zealand to the North Pacific Ocean every summer in search of food.

Record breaker

In 2007, a single bar-tailed godwit made the longest recorded non-stop flight. In nine days, it flew 7,145 miles (11,500km) from its breeding ground in Alaska to New Zealand without stopping for food or drink. By the end of its journey, the bird had lost over half its body weight. Phew!

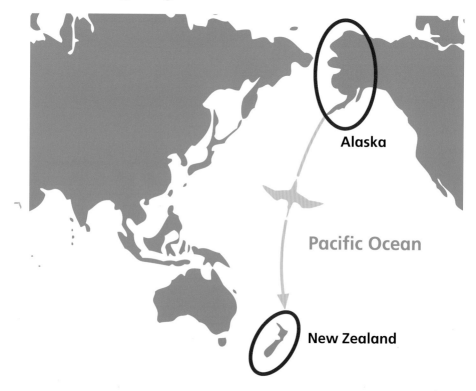

Alaska

Pacific Ocean

New Zealand

Fish old-timers

Carp

If you look after koi carp in a garden pond, they may live longer than you. Many of these fish live for 70 years – and some have made it to 200 years. A carp called Hanako was a record breaker. It died at the grand old age of 226 in 1977.

If you keep a goldfish in a bowl, how long could it live? Pet goldfish can survive for 40 years.

OLDEST GOLDFISH HAS HIS CHIPS

North Yorkshire – 1999

The world's oldest pet goldfish has died peacefully in his bowl, 43 years after he was won as a prize at a funfair.

Tish the goldfish appeared in the Guinness World Records Book. In later life, Tish faded from a bright orange colour to silver. His owner said the secret of Tish's long life was not being overfed.

The world's longest goldfish was recorded in The Netherlands in 2003. The mighty goldfish was 47.4cm from mouth to tailfin.

Reptile record

Some pet tortoises have outlived their owners. A famous giant tortoise from Galapagos lived to the grand age of 177 years old.

An Aldabra giant tortoise named Adwaita died in 2006. He was said to be 255 years old and born in 1750!

Bowhead whales

The bowhead (or Arctic) whale is the longest living mammal on Earth. Some bowhead whales have been found with the tips of spears in them from whale hunters 200 years ago.

The oldest known bowhead whale was at least 211 years old.

Oldest animal on record

British scientists found a clam living in the sea near Iceland. By counting the growth rings on its shell, they worked out its age. The clam (an ocean quahog) was 405-410 years old.

4. Super killers

What are the deadliest creatures on the planet? What kills the most humans (apart from other humans)? Even though lions, tigers, crocodiles, hippos and great white sharks kill people every year, our biggest killers are much smaller.

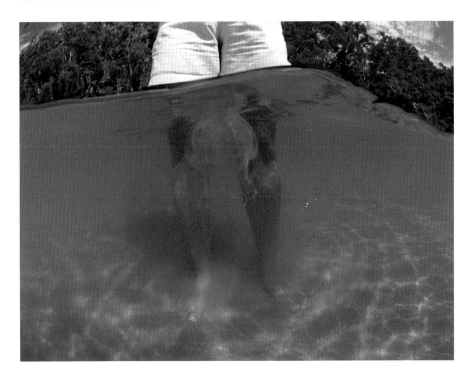

The box jellyfish (known as a sea wasp) has up to 60 tentacles, which can be up to 3 metres long. Each tentacle has 5,000 stinging cells. That's enough poison to kill 60 humans. Best to keep clear!

Venomous snakes kill thousands of people every year – maybe as many as 50,000. Asian cobras are the main culprits.

The biggest human-killers on the planet are insects. Some mosquitoes pass on malaria. This disease kills over two million people each year. The mosquito still tops the killer records.

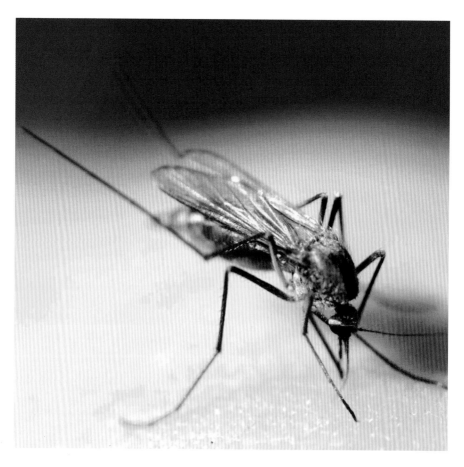

Biggest snake

The big question: which is the biggest snake in the world? An anaconda or a python?

The world's heaviest snake is the green anaconda from the swamps of South America. However, pythons have been known to grow longer. Even so, in 1944 a green anaconda over 11 metres long was found in South America – but it escaped. Now meet the longest pet python on record…

Medusa, a python of 7.67 metres, made the Guinness World Records Book in 2011. It is rare for these snakes to grow longer than 6 metres. This ten-year-old python needed 15 people to hold her to be measured. Medusa weighs 158.8kg and is fed on rabbits, pigs and deer – served whole. And yes, giant snakes have also eaten people!

Biggest spider

Very few spiders can do you any harm. Even so, one of the most common fears people have is of spiders (arachnophobia). Perhaps we would all tremble if one of the record breakers dropped on us!

The world's largest and heaviest spiders are tarantulas. The biggest of them is the Goliath bird-eating tarantula from Venezuela. It uses its large fangs (2.5cm long) to inject venom into its prey. Don't worry – if a tarantula bites you, it's no worse than a sting from a wasp.

WOW! facts

A male Goliath bird-eating spider found in Venezuela in 1965 had a leg span of 28cm. That's big enough to cover your dinner plate… or your face!

5. Super pets

Many pets have ended up in the record books. Cats and dogs have gone on record journeys.

Bobbie was a two-year-old collie. In 1923, his family took him on holiday to Indiana where they lost him. They searched for him but had to go back home to Oregon without him. They never expected to see him again. Six months later, Bobbie appeared on their doorstep! He was thin and hungry, and his feet were worn to the bone. He had walked 2,550 miles across desert, mountains and snow to reach his home in Oregon. Bobbie became world famous for his adventure.

Cats have gone on record journeys, too. In 1953, a cat called Sugar trekked 1,500 miles from California to Oklahoma. Her family left her behind with a friend when they moved house because they didn't think Sugar would cope with the long car journey. But Sugar had other plans. Fourteen months later, Sugar arrived at her owner's new house. It was big hugs all round! Sugar was a long-haired Persian cat but not quite like Colonel Meow, as you are about to see.

Colonel Meow holds the world record for the longest fur on a cat. His fur is 22.9cm long!

Longest surviving headless chicken

In 1945, farmer Lloyd Olsen of Colorado went out to get one of his chickens for dinner. He chopped off the rooster's head with an axe but the blade missed the bird's main vein and brain stem. The headless chicken wasn't dead! Lloyd called him Miracle Mike.

Mike seemed happy to sit on a perch so Lloyd fed him with an eyedropper down the neck. If Mike began to choke, Lloyd cleared his throat with the eyedropper and all was fine.

Mike was soon famous. People paid to see 'The Wonder Chicken'. Lloyd and his wife took him to shows.

Eighteen months later, in 1947, the Olsens and Mike went on tour and spent a night in a motel. Mike started choking in the night. Lloyd couldn't find the dropper and was too late to save Mike. The famous record-breaking headless pet chicken finally died.

In 2003, a film was made of this weird but true record: *Chick Flick: The Miracle Mike Story!*

Keep a look-out for the surprising animal record breakers of the future.

Index